30

Leadership!

Messages to Inspire Leaders

Todd M. Simmons

WAJBOOK PRESS

30 Days of Courageous Leadership: Messages to Inspire Leaders

Todd Simmons

Published in the U.S.A by Wajbook Press, San Antonio, Texas.

Paperback Version: ISBN 978-0-9904990-8-4

Kindle Version: ISBN 978-0-9904990-9-1

Library of Congress Control Number: 2019954531

For information about special discounts for bulk purchases, or speaking opportunities, please contact us at editor@wajbookpress.com.

The views expressed in this book are those of the author.

TABLE OF CONTENTS

Foreword

Leadership is one of the most challenging endeavors. Should you embrace this critical challenge? Should you embrace the commitment? The responsibility? Do you have what it takes?

Before you can be an effective leader, you have to know what makes you get up and tackle the challenges of the day head-on. Like most, I have personally struggled with being inspired. When I think back at what got me up, motivated, and back into the game, it was an inspirational leader who could not only see the good in me but made me believe in it.

My leader made me believe there was a leader in me. He made me believe I can make a difference. And I believe you can too. Should you embrace the challenge? Yes! Do you have what it takes? Absolutely! How do I know? Because you were drawn to this book. Your inner leader was drawn to this book.

30 Days of Courageous Leadership: Messages to Inspire Leaders

These leadership affirmations will help leaders at all levels on their journey to inspirational leadership. These messages are meant to inspire you to inspire others. Becoming an authentic leader will clear a pathway to building trusting and long-lasting relationships that will positively transform people in their organizations.

Like developing life long leadership skills, this book requires your commitment. Your first task is to commit to ten minutes every morning to read one daily lesson and contemplate how to apply it to your life. Ten minutes a day can influence the rest of your life. Commit and follow through!

Day 1

LEADERS FACE CHALLENGES HEAD ON

You can guarantee there will be adversity in your pursuit of success. There are several ways to deal with challenges as they arise. Invest in your resiliency now to build the mental toughness for the unexpected rough waters ahead.

In 2003, I was nearing the completion of my undergraduate degree. It was an exciting time as I would be the first in my family to graduate from college. My very last course was algebra. I took the course and failed. It was devastating. Four months later, I made a second attempt at a different university, which was 36 miles away from my home. I failed again. I was devastated again and did not go back to school for almost a year. But I couldn't give up completely. The third time I signed up, I changed my mindset. I spent months preparing with several tutors, making the preparation part of my daily routine, and I completed the course. This mindset taught me a valuable lesson that is with me to this day.

"Often, the only thing separating failure and success is a refusal to give up!"

Day 2

LEADERS EVALUATE THEIR CIRCLE

It is said that a person's character is primarily developed by the sum of the five people they are closest to. Evaluate your circle, and if you're surrounding yourself with people who do not challenge you with tough, thought-provoking questions, you'll never live up to your full potential to conceptualize those answers.

Seek out and surround yourself with those who inspire and challenge your mind; do not mistake verbal sparring and intellectual admiration as a threat or as a negative challenge to you personally. As a leader, I am very thankful for my accountability partners. They are integral to my circle.

"My circle should tell me what I need to hear and not what I want to hear."

Day 3

LEADERS BUILD THE TEAM THEY HAVE

Unlike the grade-school playground, we do not routinely have the opportunity to pick our team. But we do have the opportunity as leaders to shape and develop highly effective teams.

The first rule is TRUST. Trust builds RESPECT. Respect builds LOYALTY. Loyalty builds an unbreakable BOND.

Take a leap of faith. The surest way to bring out the best in your team is to believe in the best of them.

In 2009, I was placed in charge of a small section of 20 personnel. They just came off a lengthy investigation where several mid-level managers were removed. Trust in leadership had eroded to a significant point. My message was clear at our first meeting; "some of you want off this team; some of you do not have trust in me or believe I have your best interest in mind. I ask you to stay on board, help us become a team, and work at building a relationship." I finished by having everyone come to the center of the room, put all their hands in, and looked the group in the eyes, stating the phrase below. Twelve months later, we rated as the most effective section with both team and individual awards in the organization.

"All hands in... we are all in this together."

Day 4

LEADERS KEEP IT REAL

The phrase "Keep It Real" can be used in several ways. To me, keeping it real means being a deliberate and compassionate leader. Honesty, doing the right thing, genuineness, fairness, and reasonability are aspects of keeping it real.

The business world is not exempt from right and wrong boundaries. Pursuit of success does not entitle you to an "It's not personal, it's business" mentality. As a leader, you are going to work with real people with real families and real aspirations.

If you don't keep it real, you'll end up with pawns, not followers. Pawns *have* to work for you. Followers want to work for you.

"Am I keeping it real?"

Day 5

Leaders' 10 CRITICAL SECONDS

Are you a drive-by greeter?

Do you check the box with a simple hello or goodbye without a connection? It takes about 10 seconds to stop, look someone in the eye and ask: "how are you doing?" Those 10 seconds can lead to a meaningful conversation, and ultimately, a relationship of trust that can last a lifetime.

If you stop and take a second to look around you, there will be those that were invisible to you. It may be someone that you do not routinely have to communicate with but are still treasured members of the team. This can be a blind spot for leaders, especially those with complex responsibilities.

Leaders have to work hard to ensure they are making meaningful connections. You have to make those you encounter the center of attention. Do not underestimate the power of building meaningful relationships.

"How am I using my 10 seconds?"

Day 6

LEADERSHIP IS LEARNERSHIP

Leaders are learners. The easiest way to achieve growth is through knowledge.

Elevate your growth by developing a habit for reading. Expand your catalog to more than those titles of personal enjoyment and add challenging topics for personal and professional growth. When I was young, I did not have a thirst for reading and missed out on the imagination, and creativity reading helps develops.

As I grew older and traveled more around the world, I developed a thirst for reading about the different cultures of the world, and it opened my perspective on the deep rich history of the world compared to the five square miles where I was raised.

Later, as my leadership responsibilities grew in my career, leadership and resiliency became two critical topics. I had to develop the ability to turn newfound knowledge into meaningful connections, and it all started with reading.

What have you read lately? Are you sharing this knowledge with your circle?

"If you stop learning today, you stop leading tomorrow."

– Howard Hendricks

Day 7

LEADERS TRUST IN THEIR ABILITY

The view from 30,000 feet is often obscured by cloud cover. Trust your "instruments" to guide you. Don't allow temporary obstructions to limit your ability for a smooth landing. Your training, ability, and intelligence have prepared you for challenges beyond comprehension.

Due to my long-time serving in the United States Air Force, I could not resist using an aviation reference for this project. Leaders make decisions! Remember to fall back on your training...That is what I was told when I was thrust into a significant leadership position a few years earlier than expected. Simply put, leadership can be littered with uncertainty at times. Trust in your ability and have the courage to identify where you have gaps. There will be setbacks, even on your best days. Trust that you were selected for the task because someone not only saw your potential but also believed in it.

Tell yourself, "I got this! I can trust my abilities! Let's Go!"

Day 8

LEADERSHIP IS RISKY

Leadership can be tough, messy, and sometimes risky. Dr. Martin Luther King, Jr. did not retreat when the task got tough or even life-threatening. Leaders do not stay silent, even when it comes at personal risk to themselves. Dr. King exemplified these characteristics.

Dr. King, at the height of the civil rights movement, received death threats against himself and his family. He could have retreated, and no one would have looked at him with any shame. He chose to lead when it was most difficult, even if it meant sacrificing his life.

I moved to Montgomery, Alabama, in the summer of 2017. I remember taking a tour with a class to the home of Dr. King when we lived in Montgomery. I remember the tour guide explaining the incident when a firebomb was thrown on the front porch of the house while Dr. King's family was inside. He knew the risk and could have rightfully walked away that day. He did not and continued to fight for what he believed in, even at considerable risk to his family.

"What am I willing to risk?"

Day 9

LEADERS DO THE WORK

"You are doing a good job!"

That is a common phrase used throughout work centers, regardless of industry. But it's at risk of losing its meaning. Hopefully, when used, it focuses on the individual's ability to complete tasks, lead, and uphold the standards of the organization. Doing a good job is not the new hello, but rather a standard to uphold.

This message is simple: do a good job!

Today, we see a deficit in leaders or managers possessing the skills to hold those they lead accountable. It leads to ambiguous statements to shield actual performance issues. Some blame social media and our inability to connect and communicate face to face. That could be a factor, but how does that play out in business. For example: If I am a small business owner with 20 employees and not making a net profit, "you are doing a good job" is hurting your business, which will eventually hurt your employees. Having a culture of accountability where the work is being done to a high standard changes the equation. Now that statement has a direct linkage to productivity.

"Am I keeping others accountable?"

Day 10

LEADERS SET THE TONE

Become the person you want your team to emulate.

Mimic the culture you want to set in the organization. If you are not a living breathing example of the organizational culture to the best of your ability, why would anyone else feel they need to be?

Be mindful of how you dress, how you act under pressure, how you react when things go wrong. Your employees are always watching. As a leader, you need to be the example.

You need to set the tone and represent not only what your organization is, but also what you want it to be.

"Am I setting the tone for success?"

Day 11

LEADERS UNDERSTAND THE POWER OF INCLUSIVENESS

"The Power of WE"

An email from a colleague read "I" over and over again. There were numerous places where he referred to "my," "my idea," "my org," and "my plan." Words have meanings. Even when intentions are pure, our words can convey the wrong message.

When it is about "US," then "WE" matters. "I" can never accomplish anything alone.

This is an example of leadership awareness. In correspondence, speeches, office gatherings, etc., you have to ensure your communication has a tone of inclusiveness. This was a learning experience for me. I worked for 20 years in one functional specialty of the organization. I was familiar with its culture and leadership style. When I was promoted to lead the entire team, which included varied sections with their own cultures, I was unaware that the way I communicated with the entire team was alienating half of the people in the organization.

"My I needs to become We."

Day 12

LEADERS CONTINUE TO GROW

Growth can take place anywhere, at any time. The opportunity to expand your knowledge, perspective, and creativity can come from the most unexpected places.

Plants don't grow on their own. They need water. They need sunlight. They need to rely on their roots to support them. You can't rely on yourself and expect to grow.

Growth provides leaders the opportunity to expand their intellectual capacity to lead those around them better. Do not only expect growth to come from those above you. Seek out feedback and be willing to listen with an honest ear when it is given.

"Where is my growth stunted?"

Day 13

LEADERS PAY ATTENTION

Have you ever been surprised when you learn about the talents, interests, joys, sorrows, etc. from someone you routinely cross paths with? Do you say, "I didn't know that about you?" With the fast pace of life, it can be easy to overlook what's standing right in front of you.

Look beyond the mask, and you will be surprised what's hiding in plain sight.

I SEE YOU!

Depending on the size of the organization, it can be challenging to know every detail about every person you work with. However, as I have stated throughout the book, it comes down to culture. It is easy to learn something about anyone you meet. It does not have to be in-depth knowledge of who they are, but something as simple as conversing about about the new plant on the their desk. Such small gesture could lead to a relationship of trust, loyalty, and commitment.

"If I care, they will care."

Day 14

LEADERS HAVE INTEGRITY

As leaders, you WILL face challenges that can compromise your integrity or ability to lead with honor. Hold the line!

This can be the most difficult, but most important standard as a leader. It is easy to look the other way on things that go against organization culture. But going easy leads to cutting corners.

If the culture in the organization is everyone shows up on time, then everyone needs to show up on time. Including you. You set the bar, and you need to meet that bar, every time.

If you say you have integrity, then have it indeed. Leaders cannot pick and choose to exercise this characteristic.

"Integrity is never on discount."

Day 15

LEADERS BUILD TRUST

What's the bottom line? EVERYONE MATTERS!

Trust, humility and respect are the hallmarks of effective leadership and, ultimately, organizational success. Leadership is being a "human," which leads to mutual respect, believability, and trust.

I ask myself, what made me want to stay in my current career beyond my first four years? The answer is trust in my leadership. It took a leader who built trust by being human within the organization for me to truly believe I had a personal stake in the success of the organization.

Building unbreakable trust is the cornerstone of organizational success. Follow through with your promises. Admit when you make a mistake. Give credit where credit is due. By doing so, your employees will respect you, and trust you.

"Trust is the cornerstone of success."

Day 16

LEADERS ARE GOOD FOLLOWERS

Change more than your socks today!

Find ways to be better, faster, wiser, smarter, kinder, and, most importantly, a better follower.

Followership is just as crucial as leadership. As I rose through the ranks in the military and ultimately to the highest enlisted rank, followership became more critical than when I was a 19-year-old entry-level recruit.

The ability to ensure you maintain the emotional intelligence to realize rank and position does not guarantee you're the smartest person in the room is essential. The best leaders in any industry know when to step up and step back.

"I am not always the smartest person in the room, but I can always learn from them."

Day 17

LEADERS KNOW THEIR PURPOSE

Knowing your why is knowing your purpose as a leader. Every morning I get up, I reflect on what my why or purpose is for the day. As I reflect, one of the last things I do is look into the mirror right before I leave for the day (my accountability mirror). Sometimes I may say a few words of encouragement, or sometimes it may be a few seconds of silent reflection. Either way, I leave with a purpose and a better understanding of my why.

Why change?

Why be bold?

Why should you unleash them?

Why should you be passionate?

Why should you embrace innovation?

...BECAUSE you are capable! Excuses are easy, but the best results take courage!

"Why does what I do matter to me, matter to my family, and matter to my employees?"

Day 18

LEADERS BUILD CONFIDENCE

Confidence is a state of mind, which is a direct result of self-satisfaction in knowing you made an effort to do your best to become the best you can be.

Building confidence is no different than building muscles: you have to exercise it regularly.

My current position requires me to speak in front of large audiences on a routine basis. I remember a few years ago, I was not confident in my public speaking. My most memorable experience with a lack of confidence was a speaking engagement with a few hundred people in the audience. This was my first time speaking to an audience of this size and prominence. I spent 20 minutes in the bathroom sick and felt like I could not go through with the task. I looked in the mirror and said, “it is now or never.” After that event, I sought out as many speaking engagements I could. Each engagement had its challenges, and through time I built the confidence to actually enjoy the experiences.

“Confidence is an attitude!”

Day 19

LEADERS DREAM BIG

There are individuals all around you that have dreams and ambitions that some view as impossible! Dream big. Be bold enough to take risks to jump from impossible to POSSIBLE.

And you don't have to dream alone.

There will be those in your organization that have "big ideas" that are not supported by the organization. Do not shun these big thinkers. After 100 failed ideas, they may have idea number 101 that is the gamechanger.

Listen to the thoughtful, the imaginative, and the creative.

"Dream big. Dream bold. Dream together."

Day 20

LEADERS HELP DEFINE SUCCESS

Success is defined in an infinite number of ways. As a leader, you must know how you define success.

Does your subordinates' definition of success look different than yours?

How do leaders in your organization define organizational success?

I challenge you today to sit down and have that conversation with someone in your sphere of influence.

Every member of an organization defines success differently. Each member will have different backgrounds and different personal and professional goals. That makes it difficult to infuse one set of values on the masses. As a leader, it will take work to individualize your leadership style.

"Success is not an idea. It's a clearly defined goal."

Day 21

LEADERS ARE HUMBLE

We often speak, as well as in popular media, of the characteristics of "great" leaders. In my opinion, humility is number one. Humble leaders are usually the most effective leaders because they have high self-awareness.

Unfortunately, there are "me leaders" that exist in every organization. They are not focused on organization success, which means nobody is treated with the dignity and respect they deserve.

As leaders, you have to display humility in and out of the organization. This is an area that cannot be faked or failed.

"True humility is not thinking less of yourself; it is thinking of yourself less."

– Rick Warren

Day 22

LEADERS ARE SELF AWARE

Self-awareness is the conscious knowledge of one's character, feelings, motives, and desires. Once you are aware of yourself, you can become more effective in every aspect of your life. It is also easier for you to understand other people and detect how they perceive you in return.

The lack of self-awareness can be contributed to many factors. One of the major reasons I have witnessed is the lack of accountability partners, or those who are willing to give you honest feedback.

Becoming self aware begins with recognizing your own failures. Why did you fail? What aspects of your personality hindered your progress? Did you try to do something you're not good at, or didn't really care about? Then, think of your successes and ask yourself the same counterpart questions.

"My weaknesses are only weaknesses if I don't acknowledge them. Once acknowledged, I can overcome or work around them."

Day 23

LEADERS ARE ETHICAL

Ethical leaders have an impact on how people in their organizations behave and what they achieve. Ethical leadership is a must at all levels to include peer leadership.

I could provide just as many examples of unethical leadership as I could of positive examples of ethical leadership.

One example of unethical leadership is a leader eroding trust by supporting an effort in public and subverting the effort behind closed doors without telling their subordinates. This is an awful characteristic for a leader at any level and usually leads to a toxic working environment.

On the other hand, a leader who backs his employees in the office, in public, and even in front of his own superiors despite possible backlash is a leader worth following. It's the right thing to do and, in the long run, the smart thing to do because your employees will back you in return.

"An unethical leader isn't one worth following."

Day 24

LEADERS SPEAK TRUTH TO POWER

Speaking truth to power means believing deeply in what you say and fighting every day to have that heard. It may not be popular; it means taking a risk; it means standing for something.

During a staff meeting, I asked, "why do we not talk about the uptick in individuals in the organization committing suicide?" This bold statement was taken as an insult and attack on leadership culture. But it was merely ensuring this important topic was addressed and openly discussed. This became a risk to my career as I was quickly labeled a non-team player. I put others on the spot and it made them uncomfortable.

"Speaking truth to power will be uncomfortable, but its worth the risk. It's worth doing the right thing."

Day 25

LEADERS HAVE CREDIBILITY

Leaders who lack credibility will not have a positive influence on organizational culture or sucess. You have to be a leader others want to emulate before you can begin to lead effectively.

To build credibility, you need to know what you're talking about. You need to be informed. You need to show your employees that you are the real deal.

If you don't know the answer, don't act like you do. If you make a mistake, don't act like it wasn't your fault. It will devalue your credibility, and you'll ultimately lose trust and respect.

"My opinion only counts if my account is in the positive. Do not judge others when you are in overdraft."

Day 26

LEADERS ACKNOWLEDGE

Don't confuse, as many do, credit for acknowledgment. Most subordinates do not seek credit for their contributions to organizational success. They want to be acknowledged for being a valuable team member. It is a critical difference.

As a leader of a business or a process, you have to ask, what makes someone show up and give 100% to my business which ultimately benefits me, as the owner, the most? Their attitude, enthusiasm, and value to the organization are directly tied to the profitability of the company. I eat at Chick-Fil-

A for more than the chicken. I love the way they make me feel regardless if it's a dining in experience or at the drive-through.

If you say pay is what drives employees, you're wrong. I have had several job offers where the compensation would have been an influencer to some, but not when you are looking for value. Acknowledge those you lead. They are looking for more than written words saying, "good job."

"More than anything, my employees want to know they are a valued member of the team."

Day 27

LEADERS ARE UNCOMFORTABLE

Elevate your conversation IQ by seeking out those that will raise the bar on your thinking. If conversations are going over your head, you are in the right group. It means learning is occurring.

When I think about who I call for advice, I do not think about what outcome I am looking for. It can become a habit (bad habit) to call those that are usually going to agree with you.

Additionally, when looking for mental stimulation, we have a habit of seeking out the most comfortable environments.

Try changing both of these patterns by calling those that you do not usually agree with, have the ability to offer constructive feedback and those groups of people you are most unfamiliar with. It will elevate your C-IQ.

"Growth comes with growing pains."

Day 28

LEADERS DO NOT SEEK AUTHORITY

When those you lead continue their conversation uninterrupted when you enter a room, you have achieved leadership equilibrium.

Leaders have to know and understand their position. Certain privileges come with most leadership positions, but it is important not to confuse perks with privilege.

I have a private restroom in my office, but routinely walk out to the public restroom that everyone uses. Additionally, there are several parking spaces for me around the campus, but I regularly park in the first available regardless of location. Perks are great and deserved, but they can lead to an attitude that "I am in charge." Trust me; everyone already knows you are in charge.

"Leadership is a privilege, not to be taken lightly."

Day 29

LEADERS HAVE FUN

Fun is a key component in self-fulfillment and the long-term success of those you lead. If they see you smiling, there is a good chance they will also smile.

Find ways to ensure fun is incorporated into your daily organizational culture. There will never be a one-size-fits-all solution, so it is essential to be genuine and inclusive.

The most crucial aspect of fun is middle and senior leadership involvement. Your participation as a leader will set the tone.

"The less work feels like work, the more productive you can be."

Day 30

LEADERS KNOW WHEN TO TAKE A KNEE

The most important of all 30 affirmations is knowing when to "take a knee." Life should be an ultra-marathon and not a sprint. When the most important things in your life become #5, 6, 7, or 8 on your list, it is time to take a KNEE!

Leadership is not a sprint. Your best output is based on your ability to perform at the top of your game. If you have vacation time, do not bank it, take it.

Make a conscious effort to set and keep personal commitments.

"The greatest threat to success is burning out. Know when to take a knee!"

About the Author

Todd Simmons is the founder and President of Courageous Leadership Alliance.

Todd has a global reputation in leadership development. He served over 25 years in the U.S. Air Force, including assignments in both the Pacific and European regions for 17 years. His final position in the Air Force was Command Chief for Air University, where he led the professional development and education for 50,000 resident and 120,000 non-resident Air Force affiliated students each year.

He is on a mission to create a coalition of passionate leaders willing to build healthy organizational cultures. With over 25 years leading complex organizations, Todd is an authentic voice in the leadership arena– from building top-performing teams and communicating within and across cultures to achieving the best possible solutions.

Made in the USA
Middletown, DE
14 November 2021